Yes! We Can Do It!

Coty Mampeule

Copyright 2012 by Coty Mampeule

Smashwords Edition

Table of Contents

1. Start Up
2. Resources
    a. Hardware
    b. Software
    c. Connection
3. Marketing Mix
    a. Product
    b. Price
    c. Placement
    d. Promotion
4. Survey
5. Online Support

Start Up

Everybody has a story to tell. No exceptions! Have you ever looked back into your life, from as far as you can recall the events in your life, you have a great story to tell. Here is what mostly a hindrance to all of us is, *you know the story of your life and you probably think it is boring.* You *should* think it is boring because, you have listened to it your whole life. You have seen that movie of your life every second of your life. It is okay. You are one of many who believe the greatest people in life are the only chosen few to tell of their interesting lives. I am here to tell you that you are so wrong. Your life is interesting too. And you can tell a percent of computer universe and they will love to hear your story.

Think about it logically and try and take a chance. Facebook has reached a 1 billion people tally by the end of 2011, releasing their phenomenal news to the world for all to be aware. Mark Zuckerberg is a genius and so are you in your own right. All you need is to reach out within you, take a seat and write your story of the interesting things that happened in your life and make money while you are doing it. I am very sure that most of successful storytellers had an element of their personal life influencing their books and work. You may be reading this and say, well I don't have the time and it is such a work to do all that. You are saying this because it is a global phenomenon to think you can't until there's something in your life that pushes you to write something down.

Publishing News

According to the Association of American Publishers, e-books grew from 0.6% of the total trade market share in 2008 to 6.4% in 2010, the most recent figures available. Total net revenue for 2010: $878 million with 114 million e-books sold. In adult fiction, e-books are now 13.6% of the market.

As a lover of literature, grammar or any media entertainment, you can turn your love of it into a money-making vehicle. Looking at the greatest people who have done so in the past, they were driven by the love of reading. Then the passion turned into writing few things here and there. Then they went to their family members and friends to do a test run on their ability to convey their messages on paper or on print. They either used a pen, a typewriter or a computer. The most advanced method would be the computer in whatever form it is; it can break barriers and have you realize your full potential in no time.

EBooks are slowly taking over the print media inch by inch. In fact it would be incorrect to say by an inch, it has done so by a whooping mile. Talking to few publishers while I was doing a research for my book, most of them were keen to list the book as an ebook with fewer frustrations as it has a potential of reaching billions of the readers in the computer world. If you are sitting thinking you don't have time, then how is it that you have time to read a newspaper, a magazine and being on Facebook or Twitter in one day, and to top it all, you give Facebook or Twitter, 30% of your day, why, because it is exciting to hear what others have to say. In two weeks, you can write an eBook of 60 000 words. A full eBook!

Here is a newsflash for you: what you write on your Facebook wall has a fraction of your friends finding you interesting. A fraction of your friends could be 30% of your total friends. Now try to think logical for a moment, as I am here to show you facts that do not need a scientific research.

- Your friends on Facebook are, for the purpose of this exercise, say 500.

- 30% percent of your 500 friends respond to what you write on your wall. This you can check by looking at the comments at the end of that topic. Now, 30% people of 500 is 150 people.
- Using Facebook as a sample space, your audience to what you have to say is 30%. This forms a basis of what topics of your life people are interested in, or what knowledge, or what general self help or advice you can give.

Having ascertained these few facts and I say facts proudly because you too can look into it and see for yourself, try to imagine a larger sample space. Although you may think that people chat for free on Facebook and you need to sell your story, here is IN YOUR FACE reprimanding thought, Facebook limits what you can write on your wall, and a person who you are telling your little story to, is dying to hear more of it if not the rest, and some would pay you a dollar to finish it. Just a dollar, you may say. Think outside a box for little I beg you.

Let's get back to the sample space issue of 30% Facebook scenario.

Say you spent at most 30% of your day on Facebook; it would translate in breaks of few minutes culminating to a serious 6.2 hours of your day. Let me elaborate so that you are with me.

- You wake up at 06h00 and go to bed at 20h00.
- You then between lunch and tea breaks at work, spend a few moments chatting.
- Between trips to and from your work, you spend few minutes chatting too.
- At 22h00, you go to bed and spend an extra 2 hours while you are waiting to doze off.

It is now obvious that while you are hooked on Facebook, you shall be spending half the time to write a book of any topic of interest. Just 4 hours of your time, for a week or two.

Another interesting fact that needs a line of its own on this page is, are you ready to hear it, you probably write almost 6000 words on Facebook while you are chatting with your friends a day.

Yes, I said it, 6000 words and for some serious Facebook junkies, this is but a minimum. I have already spent 30 minutes on the computer and I have written 1,052 words of this book already. In four hours time, if I have enough time and less to do, I may write up to 4208 words to give me two chapters.

Resources

a) Hardware

Computer

Since this book is about showing you how you can take your minimum investment and turn it into a great return, we don't want to waste time with stories. You need an initial $500 or equivalent as per your country's currency. Say for an example if you are in the United Kingdom and your currency would be Pounds, you would need approximately 350.00 and if you are, say in South Africa, and you use Rands, you shall need 4000.00. Be free to do your own conversion using your country's currency and its rate as compared to American Dollar.

You need a writing device and a laptop is a great investment. If you have more cash you can buy the latest gadget but since we are on a tight budget, a laptop is a good start. The minimum you can spend on a good laptop is $250 new one or a newly refurbished for half the price. If you have it already, then it's a bonus. A desktop computer is fine as well if you can't have a laptop, but the latter is quite great because you can do you writing anywhere you go. One thing I can advise on is that, you shouldn't be too serious on brands. As long as you have a guarantee on your purchase and you backup your work on discs, then you have less to worry about. Peace of mind is vital before you can start operating on any business.

b) *Software*

Programs

For software on the computer itself, you need not worry about spending some money as you would need word document and these come standard with all computers. This is so obvious that I am already embarrassed to even mention it. Needless to say, I have to mention it. What if you are new into computer world environment and you are wondering what we are talking about? You shouldn't be left out.

Extra programs

As you read along, especially on the Marketing Mix part of the book, you will see why it is important to have some few extra programs to help you excel in marketing your book. I can mention minimum required programs that won't set you off from you initial investment. Think of this a business venture you are undertaking and you need to be stringent on your spent.

- You have to have a program that creates your artwork or book cover.
- You have to have a program that changes your work into multiple formats
- You have to have a program that allows an interchanges use of internet browser.

Let's explain the first point briefly.

When you put a Cover Photo on Facebook, your choice of what you put in there shall be directly proportional to the number of people requesting your friendship. The more clearly, beautiful picture you place, the more you will get friendship requests and the uglier the picture the more you will spend time asking for friends request. Look at some of your friends who have a suggestive photo on the walls and see how many friends they have. Don't go for obscene as you may lose credibility of your creative story telling work.

A great program to purchase creating eBook covers in an easy creative way is **True Box Shot Cover Editor.** It creates stunning electronic eBook covers in less than 10 minutes. Simple examples below.

  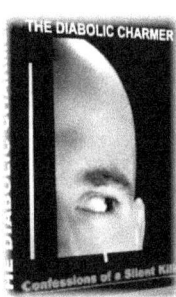

Let's go to the Second point.

Most books are accepted in a **PDF format** by publishers. Have a program that helps you do this. Mostly these programs are free to try for some time. You can write your book or books first and then covert them in that format and store them for later publishing. Remember you are running a business with limited funds here.

PayPal Account is also vital for you to have. You have an existing bank account, just simply open an account online and link it with your existing bank account. It is as free as the oxygen you breathe.

c) Connection

It is a matter of known fact that since you are opening a shop electronically, you need to go into the world of the net. There are many service providers that you can choose from in your country and they have different packages and support. All you need is to do a research on your pricing as it will affect your marketing mix in the long and be sure to choose the one that is best for you. If you are on Facebook, this must be a boring story to you, but you will begin to be surprised when you get to the Marketing Mix part of the book.

Internet Connection

The reason you need to connect is to gain access to the billions of users worldwide. I love the word, worldwide. It is a clear as daylight that you will be listing your eBook for the Global community to see and try it. The one point I will emphasize is that you have to get a reliable connectivity, with a ***broadband width***. Don't sweat to understand a broadband width as it baffles many.

Here is how I understand it. Your information is like a pallet of bricks that you need to carry and you have to deliver these bricks to a particular point. You have a truck that can carry only 1 pallet traveling on a tiny bumpy road. This will have your delivery getting to its point late.

Upgrading to a broadband, would mean, you have bought a 24 pallet truck allowing carrying more bricks and using an open road with six lanes to travel in. That's it.

Some Service Providers sell a 10 gigabyte data for a dollar and with 10 Gigs; you are set for a whole month. For example a Telkom Company in South Africa sells a 150 Gigabyte package for $150.00 and this can last you for a whole year with uploading and downloading functions. This is more like selling and buying function of an entity. Think of it as your operating costs.

Now let's recap on your resources and their cost. Remember we have $500.00

Laptop Computer	$250.00
TBS Cover Editor	$50.00
Internet Connectivity	$100.00
Grand Total	$500.00

Now we have all systems to go. We are ready to proceed. The exciting money making step.

Marketing Mix

Folks, ways of making money in the entire world, business wise that is, are similar and don't change a bit from any other in any other country. If Mars or Saturn inhabitants are operating a business, its Marketing Mix would contain of the four key elements undoubtedly. Skip the business courses; I am here to wrap it up for you in few words. You will thank me later when you account is six digits full.

Product

Bear with me if this part is taking too much of your time, or most of this book. Your product is an eBook, you say and end your sentence with a duh, it is okay because as a person who has spent four years at a university studying the processes of creating and selling products, and passed, I am justified to say duh back at you. There are millions of products in the world and only a few have proved to be outstanding. Why, you are now asking? It is because it is an offering that someone had to think of and decided to sell it out there, and followed it to the ends of the world. It may not be the best but it *will* sell.

Think of the two Cola Beverage Giants, Pepsi and Coke. They are, in some countries, sharing a 50/50 of the market. Ever thought of the fact surrounding the question, who started and why now they are both sitting on a 50/50 point? There is a saying in one of the African language: *The One who feasts last is as full as the one who feasts first.* Whether Coke or Pepsi started first, it's of no matter. There is a product out there and it's selling into every store you can ever think of.

What sells your Product to maximum heights? A great story is one of the key sellers to any product. When you go about pointing out features of your product, there are a gazillion like features on the similar product. When you consider your own personal story, it is as unique as you yourself. The secret lies in the elements of your life that you are willing to tell to others that would make your book outstanding. Your life story may be similar to that of someone in Bangladesh or in Iceland but is not quite the same. Ever wonder, when you are reading a newspaper about the War in Iraq, how a simple man in the street's experience was when everyday he sees flying roofs of his neighborhood and people exploding next them most of the time? Now think of how many people would want to listen to him.

Have an angle.

Most stories, even the biographies, have an element of Fiction in them. Put bluntly, the authors choose an angle that would excite the readers. He doesn't lie but he puts his story in a fictitious manner to accommodate his angle of the story. Fiction is a great way to start writing a book. You choose what suits the truth about your book, to be a perfect masterpiece. Someone who is creating something does so with a lot of imaginary scenes in his/her mind. Let's call it wishful thinking coming to reality through creation.

Blend your story.

A product's ingredients also tell a story. Think of the Master Blender in his quarters, taking every single malt whiskey and blending his creation to a blissful renowned drink. The drink in time will have a story to tell. A wine connoisseur would also appreciate the story the wine is telling him through its taste. When the wine was created, it was a fraction of other wines blended into a full flavored aromatic masterpiece of a blend. Blending in a true sense would be taking some elements of your true life experience and take a huge portion of fiction and blend the two, adding some few extracts of time real events and throwing them in. that way, you make the story much more informative of your surrounding which allows the reader to walk with you in the path, exploring your unknown world that you are revealing to him. A certain prominent figure mentioned here and there would keep a reader glued to your pages in awe and excitement. Ever heard of a movie critic that has directed a blockbuster movie? Think about it, the reason why you are your own great author, is because you have read countless books and you have had your own suggestions as to how you could have written better or presented in a certain angle with your own blending.

Here is a strong example.

How many times have you been in sticky situations and have wished you could have done something about in a different manner? Think of those and be a hero of your own movie, and write about the way you would like your reader to hear of them. Fiction blended with a few sprinkles of the truth and baked in your own oven for a delight of your readers. As a start, you don't want to be *Dan Brown* and try to write a well researched book like *The Da Vinci's Code*. You are in the beginners chair with an aim of making money doing what you love. Don't just write the book, you should begin with an end in mind. Facebook is for fun, and writing eBooks is for profit making and you are trying to aim for a $1 million dollar paycheck remember?

Stay with me here.

Have Varietals of Offerings.

Your life is also a blend of elements making you who you are. With your offering, have something extra to offer. Pepsi sells Cola, but there is Mirinda, Gatorade, Mountain Dew, Light, and the whole lot more. Coca Cola has its offerings too, they offer a wide variety of products and list them in every store for maximum profit realization. This again gives them an edge to provide consumers with choice. Do the same after your first book. This helps you to stay competitive and versatile.

Let's do a quick recap on product issue.

- Have an Angle
- Blend
- Offer more than one

Check what categories there are in book writing vocabulary. You have a lot to choose from according to your passion. It could be the following:

- Fiction
- How to
- Reference
- Religious
- And many more.

Price

The ever sensitive issue of them all in the whole world is: How much? The Price to the Commodity is mostly determined by what operating costs you have incurred. Although it depends to what you are selling, I want to reiterate a known fact: The more you sell, the more you make money when you Price is Right.

Let's think logically. You are spending a $500.00 and investing at least 4 hours of your everyday to make a whooping million dollars. If you are employed right now, take your whole salary and try to find out how much you are rating per hour. Then see if you will be able to make a million by year end.

Say you are employed as a Manager and you earn a cool $2500.00

Your workdays are from Monday until Saturday.

You simply, for this exercise sake, divide $2500.00 by 27 days. That gives you a good $92.59c a day.

You work from 09h00 to 17h00 a day which gives you 8 hours as per the law in most countries. This gives you a figure of $11.57c an hour.

Now let's look at your product and see what could influence the price.

We are talking $500.00 investment with a possible return of $1million dollars and more. You need to consider your time spent per day or month on the computer to set up your price, right? No!

You look at the right competing entry price level in the market. These are normally set from as little as $0.99c to a certain pricing of your choice. To price your book right would prove beneficial to you in the long run. Remember this is a business in a form of investment. In a business world, we would visit a number of Variables and Fixed Costs to come to your Pricing Determinants. With an eBook, this is what makes it to be more exciting. You do not have serious overheads to think and worry about. Here are few facts to ponder.

- You can list on most sites for free
- You can publish for free
- You can have an ISBN for free
- You can join other helpful sites for free
- You can advertize your eBook for free
- You can make changes and updates for free.

The only element of cash spent you incur, is buying of data bundles and if you use them for the ebook business sparingly, 10 Gigs can last you for at least two months. This information above tells you that you don't need to price your books exorbitantly. Besides, you have already invested your $500.00 which includes data bundles to last you the entire one and half year, if uncapped, and the only thing that you would dedicate to selling of the book, is time.

For a better understanding on price, here are some few tips and recommendations:

- Fiction with 60 000 words or equivalent to 100 A4 pages, should be **less than $5.00**
- How to eBooks with 60 000 word, a series of researches done on the subject and a lot of work being put in, should be **at least $5.00 or more**.
- Guidance books of 60 000 words and less should be free or be sold at a minimum attracting price of $0.99c
- Photo albums and entertaining stories are mostly for free to help market yourself.

Placement

Let's go back to my favorite beverage story. The success of both Beverage Giants is placed on two main areas.

To have a product in every part of the globe in a right condition, and

To have a constant reminder that the product does exist.

Placing your product is very vital in any business entity or corporate. Your book shall be of no exception. You have to consider the correct distribution channels. Some of them are expensive and requires a fee to sign up, but remember our quest here. We shall only consider those that are free. Consider Google Search engine for example, it is used worldwide and has many affiliating partners around the globe. Listing your book on Google Bookstore is free. How wonderful is that. You can have no costs to list your book on one of the most used Search Engine. For free.

Now let's consider this reality check for a minute, 'I invest $500.00 and hope that in time it will give me a million'. Yes We can. This means you need to sell a lot of books to achieve this. Here is my thinking, if someone has sold a million copies of a single eBook in 5 months, why do you think you are of less quality? If you take your calculator, it clearly tells you that he was selling 800 copies an hour.

Let's dig a bit deeper on this issue, and look at how we can do it too. Computers are used by millions people worldwide and the market as we have seen on the attached publication is that there are 114 million books sold. This doesn't tell us that who sold how many books, but it is a figure that is holistic. Let's look at this one person selling a million copies, and make a few observations of our own and then we can see how we shall do it too.

If he sold 1 million, then the figure changes from 114 to 113 millions, which also tells you that the market is still open to new entries, in fact whole new entries. If you are not one of those people right now, you are seriously losing out. This should give you enough gumption to start writing your own story. Enough said on the matter, I think we all get the point.

When you take your time and consider the table below, you can see the reality of selling few books in a matter of a year if you think it's difficult, but let's stick to the point of someone doing it in 5 months; you can also have the opportunity to do the same.

The table shows a minimum of 50 free sites that can list your book for free.

#	Website Address	Sites	Annum Sales	Month	Day	$ Price	Total/Store
1	www.ebookbay.com	eBookBay	4000	334	11	5	20000
2	www.kdpamazon.com	Amazon	4000	334	11	5	20000
3	www.lulu.com	Lulu.com	4000	334	11	5	20000
4	www.thecontentbazaar.com	Content	4000	334	11	5	20000
5	http://books.google.com	Google	4000	334	11	5	20000
6	www.smashwords.com	Smashwords	4000	334	11	5	20000
7	www.xlibris.com	xlibris	4000	334	11	5	20000
8	www.ebooksnbytes.com	eBooks n Bytes	4000	334	11	5	20000
9	www.virtual-ebooks.com/dir	Virtual Ebooks	4000	334	11	5	20000
10	www.ebooktags.com	EbookTags	4000	334	11	5	20000
11	www.ecourseweb.com	Ecourse Web	4000	334	11	5	20000
12	www.free-ebooks.net	Free eBooks	4000	334	11	5	20000
13	www.ideamarketers.com	Idea Marketers	4000	334	11	5	20000
14	www.1chapterfree.com	1Chapter Free	4000	334	11	5	20000
15	www.buy-ebook.com	Buy-Ebook	4000	334	11	5	20000
16	www.ebook.ebook2u.com	Ebook2u	4000	334	11	5	20000
17	www.ebookfriends.com	Ebookfriends	4000	334	11	5	20000
18	www.ebookpalace.com	Ebook Palace	4000	334	11	5	20000
19	www.ebookgiveaways.com	Ebookgiveaway	4000	334	11	5	20000
20	www.ebookheaven.co.uk	Ebook Haven	4000	334	11	5	20000
21	www.jogena.com	Jogena	4000	334	11	5	20000
22	www.knowbetter.com	Know Better	4000	334	11	5	20000
23	www.mindlikewater.com	Mind Like Water	4000	334	11	5	20000
24	www.published.com	Published.com	4000	334	11	5	20000
25	www.e-bookdirectory.com	The Ebook Dire	4000	334	11	5	20000
26	www.sharejunction.com	Shareware Junc	4000	334	11	5	20000
27	www.wisdomebooks.com	Wisdom Ebook	4000	334	11	5	20000
28	www.ebookleads.com	Ebook Lead	4000	334	11	5	20000
29	http://greatauthorsonline.co	Great Authors C	4000	334	11	5	20000
30	www.fictionwise.com	Fictionwise	4000	334	11	5	20000
31	www.ebookmall.com	Ebook Mall	4000	334	11	5	20000
32	www.etext.net/	Etext	4000	334	11	5	20000
33	www.ebook-india.com	Ebook-India	4000	334	11	5	20000
34	www.rkphunt.com/directory.	Hunts Ebook	4000	334	11	5	20000
35	www.bob-e-books.com	Bob-e-books	4000	334	11	5	20000
36	www.americane-books.com	American Eboo	4000	334	11	5	20000
37	www.ebookjungle.com	Ebook Jungle	4000	334	11	5	20000
38	www.awe-struck.net	Awe Struck Boc	4000	334	11	5	20000
39	http://booklocker.com	Booklocker	4000	334	11	5	20000
40	http://cyberread.com	CyberRead	4000	334	11	5	20000
41	http://www1.buyitsellit.com/	Buyit-Sellit	4000	334	11	5	20000

	Website	Name					
42	www.blish.com	Blish	4000	334	11	5	20000
43	www.ebookbroadcast.co	Ebook Broadcast	4000	334	11	5	20000
44	http://free-online-novel	Free Online Novel	4000	334	11	5	20000
45	www.e-library.us	E-Library	4000	334	11	5	20000
46	www.ebooksportal.org	Ebooks Portal	4000	334	11	5	20000
47	www.bowindex.com	BowIndex	4000	334	11	5	20000
48	www.ebookdirectory.co	Ebook Directory	4000	334	11	5	20000
49	www.free-book.co.uk	Free -Ebook	4000	334	11	5	20000
50	www.kalahari.net	Kalahari.net	4000	334	11	5	20000
Total				*200000*			*1000000*

For a clearer understanding lets visit every column individually.

Website Address column helps you identify the address of your sites your book is listed on. Think of it in terms of Book Stores or Libraries that keep your books in stock. If you were running a distribution company, then your products will be placed in these stores, for a greater reach. You would send your distributing truck to fill these stores with products. With an eBook business, your product is software that is downloadable to these sites servers. Once you have listed your book, like Wal-Mart, there's a price associated with selling your product.

The nicest of the business approach is that they take your stock on credit. Then they sell your stock at a price determined by you, and all they do is to charge you their fee to sell on your behalf. Let's explore, shall we?

Amazon lists your book at $5.00

They sell your book at $5.00

With selling to them, there a fee for conclusion of marketing and distribution to their affiliating partners.

Amazon manages to sell a book and charges you a 30% fee and gives 70%.

Basically they charge you $1.50c to sell and market your product.

Rationally again would be emphasized that when you do your pricing, look at the volume factor than the amount of work you may have done. The more you list in many stores, for free, the quicker you will realize your $Million Goal. Like any other investment, this business would need you invest in time, but if you do your marketing correctly, results may be quicker than anticipated. Moreover, the real investment of $500.00 with your bank, assuming an interest of 10.00pa will give you an extra amount of $50.00 in a year. So as to speak frankly, your total money would be $550.00 by the end of the year. You'd be grateful on the advice you took on purchasing this book. In fact a mere sale of 100 books gives you back your whole amount, so be very aware on the price you charge on your book.

The second column is the name of your Book Store. There are thousands of Book Stores and the more you discover the more you earn. I have given you fifty already, but you can add as many as you like, but keep track of your book sales. With every store, there is a small store the big store is affiliated with, so your book is distributed deeper into the market where you cannot get to.

Third column is Sales per Store per Year. Remember we are showing you the limitless endeavor that is open to you where the world of eBook readers stretches to. To understand where we took a figure of 4000 units from, let's run through it together:

Remember we said we could turn an initial investment of $500.00 into $1Million; now let's consider this then,

You need a $1million turnover and you have a distribution channel of 50 stores.

Your price is $5.00 per unit.

1000000 in dollars divided by the selling price of $5.00,

That gives you 200 000 units to sell.

Divide these units by 50 stores which you'd have the book listed in.

One store needs to sell at least a minimum of 4000 units. Remember that someone sold 1 million copies. This guy was selling 200 000 copies a month.

The fourth column shows you the monthly sales per store. You simply take the amount of targeted sales per store and divide it by a month. It has to be a month and 24 hours on the day and seven days a week. These stores are always open and are situated in worldwide website. So possibilities are great. If you look at all the cities listed on your phonebook, you will realize that you can have your book being viewed by someone in a remote area of Afghanistan, as long as he has a computer and can connect to the net. By checking exactly, you will realize that opening a groceries store at the corner of your street limits you to about 1000 per day if you are lucky. When you list your book on the net, you are guaranteed to have at least 30% of the world's population looking at your work. We are talking at minimum, 300 million or 30% who are using Facebook. Imagine if we were to talk about the total 30% of the global users?

The fifth column gives you an idea on how many units per store by day. Your minimum sales target is 200 000 to realize your goal. One store needs to sell 11 books a day. If a sale of 1 book exceeds 6 666 units, with 277 books sold per hour, 4 books per minute, what would make 11units a day impossible?

The sixth column is the price per book. Your chance of reaching your target sooner, is the inclusion of other work you might have done. If your work consists of four fiction books of 100 pages and more, obviously you will realize turnover four times greater.

$5.00 x 4 = $20.00 and this would make you $4 Million Dollar richer, with initial investment of $500.00.

The seventh and final column shows you the stores total contribution in $ terms.

The column can be to tag your sales as you would only click on the address and voila, there is a store opened for you.

Promotions

Do you know of *Coca-Cola Marketing Blunder*?

This is one story every Marketing or Business Professor likes to tell in Awe. The reason as we earlier mentioned of the two Giants being on a 50/50 parity, is the fact of the *Coke Company* being a little, as my professor would say, "corky". The company saw a huge success with their sales, and everything was going very well. Someone was having so much fun that he advised the Marketing Department to relax their spent on Promotions and Marketing of the products. The big idea was that their products are now known and it's going to take a miracle for a consumer to forget them. Well, they were wrong and this blunder caused them a great deal of market share. Other groups capitalized on this mistake and the market share for Coca-Cola became less and less in time. It took them millions of dollars to regain the market share, and Pepsi never backed down on their stand. Till this day, they are fighting neck on neck, head to head.

To have your book in every store is not enough. You need to take care of your book sales and promotions. The market is always evolving and new trends are introduced every minute. The sites or what we have referred as the book stores do their part to move sales of your book, but that is still not enough. Now you are beginning to think this is difficult, as you thought it was an easy task. We said yes you can do it but we didn't say it was going to be a walk in the park.

You can make a WALK IN THE PARK by spending at least an hour doing promotion on other sites too. Let's look at YouTube as an example for promoting your book. You just said WHAT, right?

I personally do not see any better way to promote your book in any other fashion. The most watched YouTube video is about two infants sitting and the smaller child biting the older child's finger. To me this is quite hilarious and that's it. Hilarious that a 2 minute video with no money making idea has reached a tally YouTube can't comprehend, and also hilarious because it is quite funny. YouTube promotes any video you can imagine. What is also annoying about other excited people is that they use meaningful titles to do useless things just to irk people. Use YouTube in a meaningful way.

People no longer use Google Search Engine to check what the latest movie is, even if they do, Google would direct them to YouTube to see a trailer of the movie. That's promotion at its best and YouTube is a channel to go to. For the purpose of this book and to cut too much time on many things you need to consider, I strongly suggest you open a Google Account and affiliate with Google Adsense, Google Bookstore and Google AdWords programs. It's free also.

How do you do this?

After signing up for a free account, you can register with YouTube to post your videos. You may have as many video posted on YouTube, but please, I beg you, do not falsify any information as to what people should expect. The video title must be about the video.

To create a video, quite contrary to popular belief is a cheap as buying a suit with no tag. All you need is to have a camcorder. You don't need to buy it; you can simply borrow it from friends and do a stunning video of you promoting your book. If a camcorder is too much for you, your computer comes with an inbuilt Windows Movie Maker Program. Is it free? Of course it's free.

You can download pictures to describe your book in a picture story. Here is what you need to do.

- Create a storyline of your book. Use your short description of the book.
- Download picture images from Google. The pictures must correspond with what you are saying.
- Use Windows Movie Maker to plot the story and use effects and transitions that comes with the program.
- Wrap up the story by adding a narration to it. You can use a microphone and the feature is on Windows Movie Maker.
- Post your video on your channel.
- Review your channel viewing every week for easy promotion on your adverts.

Survey

Every day, you can spend an hour on your work and chase the numbers using an excel sheet with all your website addresses, with YouTube included. Do a tally every weekend and just keep track.

Online Support

There are quite a number of other ways to promote your books too. These are:

- Own website which is free.
- Own blog site which is free.
- Affiliation Programs like ClickBank which comes with a minimal fee.
- Vendor Programs like Pay DotCom which also comes with a minimal fee.
- Google AdSense Program which is free.
- Facebook page which is free.
- Twitter page which is also free.

And these are just a few that are meaningful and you spend less time on them.

Create a website for your entire **How to eBooks**. Also create a blog and encourage people to comment.

Let's see how far we have come by recapping all of the wok in schematic fashion.

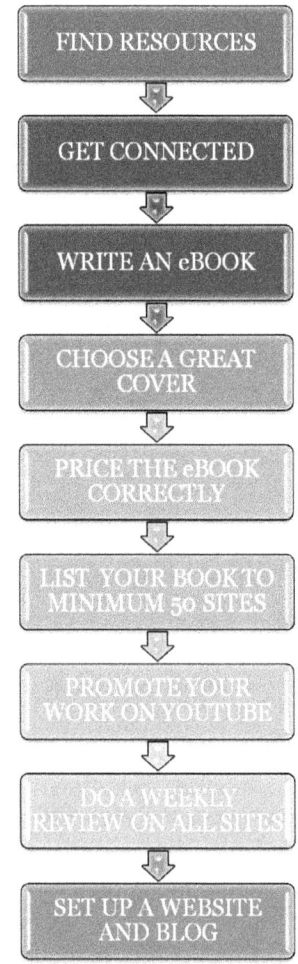

The Author

COTY MAMPEULE

His Other Renown Work...

My dream My key

"In your dreams, you are in a hospital. A Chinese Nurse is standing next to you with a healthy plate of Steak and some boiled Eggs. While you are smiling at her, suddenly she takes out a Gun and tries to shoot you; she Accidentally shoots a passerby next to your ward."

You wake up very sweaty and you start to realize that this was actually a nightmare. You get out of bed and prepare to go to work. On your way, you stop to place the numbers for a $245 Million Power-Ball. You consider your dreams and you place the following numbers:

34, 12, 36, 3, 14, 10

The next morning you check your ticket, you jump up with joy because you have won the US biggest Power-Ball. But you are not surprised because you learnt that

- a Chinese is number *(12)*,
- a Nurse is number *(14)*,
- Steak or Meat is number *(34)*,
- Eggs is number *(10)*,
- Accident is number *(3)*
- and a Gun is number *(36)*.

Learn to unlock the power of your dreams by converting images into lucky numbers and try them on lotto or power-ball games. You will be amazed how your dreams can make you rich.

THE DIABOLIC CHARMER

Inspired by the events of the Author's real life, this fictitious novel is a must read for all...

In a Corporate World where deceit, lies, conspiracy and backstabbing is rife, for most young black graduate executives, this is a world which their lecturers and professors didn't prepare them for.

Young, sweet, angelic, handsome and very charming, Coty Martins (KC) grew up in a township called Evaton, Gauteng, South Africa. Like many other black kids in his country, odds were against him to make it to the university level, let alone to work for a second largest brewery in the world. His dream was realized two years after obtaining his degree.

Entering a world of fierce competition, greed, evil scheming and greater fight for recognition, his nobility of character, his well looked after Grandeur, was tarnished and his lifelong dream he cherished with his childhood friend, Ali Nene, was ransacked before it even blossomed into a fruitful return for his 19 years investment. Like a dog with tucked tail behind its hind feet, he was defamed and reduced to nothing, his rights to a perfect life, were infringed.

With him being violated emotional by the cruel bosses and their ever loyal snitches, KC was turned from a God fearing young man, to a monster who sought to eliminate his enemies.

Using his charm and innocent looks, he lured them into a trap and effaced them one by one. His quest for revenge turned him into the most effective Silent Killer the world has ever come to know.

Consequentially he became...The Diabolic Charmer!

YES! WE CAN DO IT.

A fun way to invest in your writing talents and your computer and make money writing eBooks.

This ebook shows you how you, in 9 easy steps, can have an investment that can provide great returns.

It follows the research the author has done using his Marketing Flair, his Sales experience and his BCommerce qualification to show you how you can do it and yet spending less time on your computer.

MESSIAH ON THE RUN

'Themba Dube is a young man who is born with a miracle substance in his body. He is here in Johannesburg from Witbank, Mpumalanga. We took liberty at looking at his unique circumstances and we are about to hear the lab interim report from Privanni Jhadda, to see how each one of us can attempt to copy this natural vile.

Once this is done, we will mass produce the substance and a greatest discovery would be accredited to Alabaster Pharmaceutical Corporation. These are the exciting times for us and this is the moment you should be glad that you are working for this company. Soon you will be making history and headlines internationally.' Angelica Stone, Chief of Research says with a broad smile.

With a Pharmaceutical Corporation failing to capture him to harvest on his fluids, the Government hunting him for murder he didn't commit, a jealous pathologist wanting him dead, a rich mobster who has a heavily infected dying girl in his care, searching for him, and a martial arts expect Indian lady protecting him, the young man's life has turned into a nightmare.

Through thrilling escapes and truth finding missions, Themba Dube finds his normal life being changed dramatically, running away from almost everyone. Protecting him is his newly found love, a beautiful Privanni Jhadda, an Indian pathologist, who defies her boss's orders, to do what is right; she fights tooth and nail for her Black Prince.

But her White secret admirer supervisor, Carter James, wants the Messiah dead at all costs, and her brother's boss, Black Mobster, Jackie Khumalo taking care of his late partners White adopted daughter Thandie Bloom, suffering from Aids, the chase is mind boggling and filled with deceit, and mystery.

Can Themba and Privanni outsmart everyone?

Can the Hired Killer, the Private Eye, the Bossy and heartless Angelica Stone, the Government Agents, the Minister of Health and Jackie Khumalo get to him that easily?

Can The Messiah On The Run have enough time to save his sister from dying of Aids?

Will he be captured by Alabaster and be used as a lab subject for the rest of his life?

www.ingramcontent.com/pod-product-compliance
Lightning Source LLC
Chambersburg PA
CBHW061523180526

45171CB00001B/315